Newport Community Learning
and Libraries

Z819241

D0529113

GAY PEOPLE
Who Changed History

Adam Sutherland

WAYLAND

Newport Community Learning & Libraries	
Z819241	
PETERS	01-Oct-2015
J920.008	£8.99

First published in paperback in 2015 by Wayland
Copyright © Wayland 2015

All rights reserved.

ISBN 978 0 7502 8389 2
Library eBook ISBN 978 0 7502 8609 1
10 9 8 7 6 5 4 3 2 1

MIX
Paper from responsible sources
FSC® C104740
www.fsc.org

Editor: Nicola Edwards
Designer: Tim Mayer, MayerMedia

Wayland is an imrpint of Hachette Children's Group
Part of Hodder & Stoughton
Carmelite House
50 Victoria Embankment
London EC4Y 0DZ

An Hachette UK company

www.hachette.co.uk
www.hachettechildrens.co.uk

Picture acknowledgements
Cover: Jason Kempin/WireImage/Getty Images; title page: Terry O'Neil/Getty Images; p2 Justin Sullivan/ Getty Images; p4 Getty Images; p5 (t) Diana Davies, © New York Public Library, (b) S Bukley/Shutterstock.com; p6 Napoleon Sarony; p7 Gregory Sprague Collection, Chicago Historical Society; p8 David Shankbone; p9 Catherine McGann/Getty Images; p10 Roger Higgins; p11 François Lochon/Gamma-Rapho via Getty Images; p12 STF/AP/Press Association Images; p13 Justin Sullivan/Getty Images; p14 David, Washington DC; p15 Karl Gehring/Denver Post via Getty Images; p16 Danny W; p17 Spencer Platt/Getty Images; p18 Clive Brunskill/ ALLSPORT/Getty Images; p19 S Bukley/Shutterstock. com; p20 Terry O'Neil/Getty Images; p21 FilmMagic; p22 (tl) AP/Press Association Images, (bl) Matt Todd/AP/ Press Association Images, (ml) AP/Press Association Images, (mb) Matt Buck, (tr) Dan Savage

The website addresses (URLs) and QR codes included in this book were valid at the time of going to press. However it is possible that contents and addresses may have changed since the publication of this book. No responsibility for any such changes can be accepted by either the author or the Publisher.

CONTENTS

Words in **bold** can be found in the glossary on page 24.

Making History

Brave steps

One of our earliest history makers, Henry Gerber (page 7), even spent time in a mental institution as homosexuality was classified as a mental illness right up until 1973.

Gerber risked his freedom to form America's first homosexual organization, the Society for Human Rights, in 1924. Larry Kramer (page 8) followed in Gerber's footsteps, eventually founding the campaigning group ACT UP. Kramer's direct actions helped raise awareness of AIDS, and forced the US government to increase medical funding for people living with the disease.

In 1967 the British government **decriminalized** homosexual acts between men over the age of 21. However, US laws varied state by state, and it wasn't until 2003 – just a few years ago – that the US Supreme Court banned the remaining anti-gay laws across the United States. Today, homosexuality is still illegal in about 70 countries – that's around 35%, or more than a third of the world.

The fact that until fairly recently in Britain, and in certain US states, sexual relationships between two men or two women were illegal and punishable by prison should give a sense of the kind of fear and suspicion that homosexual people have had to live with from one day to the next. Gay people were unable to form groups, find places to socialize, or share affection with a member of the same sex without the risk of arrest, or violence.

Oscar Wilde (left), pictured in 1893 with his lover, Lord Alfred Douglas. The pair were separated when Wilde was sent to prison.

A changing world

The 1960s saw the birth of the gay liberation movement, and gay rights, with many lesbians and gay men 'coming out' and publicly declaring their sexuality. Gay communities began to grow and flourish around the world. Nevertheless, even in modern cities like New York City, there was virtually nowhere where homosexuals could legally meet to drink and dance. The police raid of the Stonewall Inn (page 16) and the riots it sparked, were directly responsible for massive steps forward in the fight for gay and lesbian rights.

Up to date

In many ways, the world is changing. Today, homosexual performer Sir Elton John (page 20) uses his worldwide profile to raise money for AIDS research through his Elton John Foundation. And US comedienne Ellen DeGeneres (page 19) 'came out' live on television. On the flip side, though, young gays and lesbians are still discriminated against and even murdered for their sexuality, or driven to suicide because of prejudice and fear. Dan Savage's It Gets Better Project (page 22) aims to provide support to educate and inspire. The hope is to continue the advances towards equality for gay people which were begun by the people in these pages.

The Stonewall Inn, site of the riot that laid the foundation for modern gay rights.

Ellen DeGeneres (right) and her wife, actress Portia de Rossi.

Oscar Wilde
Brilliant mind

Oscar Wilde was one of the most brilliant, witty and **flamboyant** playwrights of the Victorian era. A lover of aesthetics – the study and appreciation of beauty – Wilde was drawn to the homosexual world in his writing, which critics sometimes called 'unclean' and 'poisonous'. Nevertheless, in 1884, he married Constance Lloyd, and the couple had two sons.

> 66 I wanted to eat of the fruit of all the trees in the garden of the world. 99
>
> *Oscar Wilde*

Name: Oscar Fingal O'Flahertie Wills Wilde

Born: 16 October 1854 in Dublin, Ireland

Died: 30 November 1900 in Paris, France

Achievements: One of the UK's most popular playwrights. Author of 'The Picture of Dorian Gray' (1890), and 'The Importance of Being Earnest' (1895).

Interesting fact: A keen boxer, Wilde once single-handedly fought off an attack by four fellow students at Oxford University.

Oscar Wilde loved to dress and act flamboyantly.

In prison

When Wilde entered into a relationship with Lord Alfred Douglas, in 1891 (see page 4) the young man's father publicly accused Wilde of homosexuality. Wilde unwisely took him to court for libel (saying something that wasn't true). When Wilde lost, he not only had to declare himself **bankrupt**, but was also jailed for 'gross **indecency**' with other men. After two years in prison, Wilde moved to France where he lived in poverty for the rest of his life. He died of cerebral meningitis at just 46.

Henry Gerber
Gay rights pioneer

Dittmar emigrated to the United States in 1913, settling in Chicago, home to a large Germany community, and changing his name to Henry Gerber. The young Gerber was briefly committed to a mental institution because of his homosexuality, before enlisting in the US Army when America declared war on Germany.

Inspiration

As part of his time in the army Gerber spent three years back in Germany. There he became inspired by the work of German gay rights activist Magnus Hirschfeld's Scientific-Humanitarian Committee, and their attempts to reform anti-homosexual German law. Back in the US, Gerber was determined to found a similar organization.

Reaching out

In 1924, Gerber formed the Society for Human Rights and its newsletter, *Friendship and Freedom*, 'to combat public prejudice' and 'protect the interests of [abused] people'. Unfortunately, Gerber and his colleagues were arrested, and defending himself in court cost him his life savings. In 1927 he re-enlisted in the army where he ran a pen pal service called 'Connections' until 1945. He continued to write for magazines and had pieces published that promoted the cause of gay rights.

Name: Joseph Henry Dittmar

Born: 29 June 1892 in Bavaria, Germany

Died: 31 December 1972 in Washington DC, United States

Achievements: Founded the Society for Human Rights (SHR), the first known homosexual organization in the United States, and the first homosexual publication.

Interesting fact: The apartment where Gerber founded the SHR was designated a Chicago landmark in 2001.

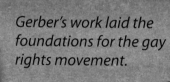

Gerber's work laid the foundations for the gay rights movement.

MAKING HISTORY

Gerber's courage inspired the growth of **LGBT** rights organizations worldwide. The better-known Mattachine Society, founded by Harry Hay in Los Angeles in 1950, took its lead from the Society for Human Rights.

Larry Kramer

Early AIDS activist

Name: Larry Kramer

Born: 25 June 1935 in Bridgeport, Connecticut, USA

Achievements: Co-founder of the Gay Men's Health Crisis (GMHC) in 1980, founder of the AIDS Coalition To Unleash Power (ACT UP) in 1987.

Interesting fact: In 2001, Kramer gave US$1m to Yale University to fund a program of gay and lesbian studies.

When members of the community began getting ill in 1980, Kramer invited a large group of gay friends to listen to a doctor who told them their illnesses were all related, and needed researching. Kramer and friends founded the Gay Men's Health Crisis (GMHC), which became the most important fund-raising and support organization for people with Acquired Immune Deficiency Syndrome (AIDS) in the New York area.

As a student at prestigious Yale University in the early 1950s, Larry Kramer attempted suicide because he felt like 'the only gay student on campus'. When he recovered, he decided to dedicate his life to fighting 'for gay people's worth'.

Early awakenings

After university, Kramer started work at Columbia Pictures, and worked his way up to the script department. In 1970 he was nominated for an Oscar for the screenplay of DH Lawrence's novel *Women in Love*. By the end of the 1970s, he was living on Fire Island in New York, which was home to a **thriving** homosexual community.

Kramer, who is living with HIV, is an outspoken supporter of safe sex.

Kramer's direct campaigning style kept HIV/AIDS at the centre of the US medical debate.

Fighting for change

Kramer increasingly felt that GMHC should actively protest for funding – violently, if necessary – and by 1983 he was forced out of the group. By 1987 he had founded the AIDS Coalition to Unleash Power (ACT UP), a direct action protest group that targeted government agencies and large companies, to publicise the lack of treatment and funding for people with AIDS.

Kramer was arrested dozens of times, but his direct action helped the organization spread across the country, raised awareness of AIDS, and improved medical funding for people living with the disease. According to **immunologist**

Anthony Fauci, 'There is no question in my mind that Larry helped changed medicine in [America]. And he helped change it for the better.'

MAKING HISTORY

The direct action protests of ACT UP are credited with changing public health policy in the United States, allowing better access to life-saving medication. Kramer also helped to raise awareness of AIDS and improve how people living with the disease were perceived.

Truman Capote
Literary sensation

Truman Capote overcame an unhappy, isolated childhood to become one of the world's best-known writers. Although he never became fully involved in the growing gay rights movement, by embracing homosexual themes in his work and living openly as a gay man, he became an important representative of the gay community throughout the 20th century.

School years

Neglected by his mother and father, Capote spent much of his childhood living with relatives in the Deep South of the United States. He was bullied by schoolmates, and even his mother, for his high-pitched voice and

Name: Truman Streckfus Persons

Born: 30 September 1924 in New Orleans, Louisiana, USA

Died: 25 August 1984 in Palm Springs, California, USA

Achievements: Two Edgar Allen Poe writing awards – for 'The Innocents' (1962) and 'In Cold Blood' (1966)

Interesting fact: Capote was a childhood friend of Harper Lee and was the inspiration for the character of Dill in her novel 'To Kill A Mockingbird'.

Capote was inspired to write 'In Cold Blood' by a 300-word article he read in the New York Times.

effeminate gestures and was sent to a military academy to 'make him more masculine'.

Writing career

Capote enjoyed huge success with his novel *Breakfast at Tiffany's*, which was made into an award-winning film, and his non-fiction study of the murder of a Kansas family *In Cold Blood*. In his later life, he because addicted to drugs and alcohol, and died of liver disease at the age of just 59.

> " I don't care what anybody says about me as long as it isn't true. "
>
> *Truman Capote*

Andy Warhol
Art genius

The son of a Slovakian coal miner, Andy Warhol grew up to become one of the world's most talked-about artists. Often drawing on images from gay underground culture, Warhol's own homosexuality strongly influenced his work. His openly gay lifestyle, before the birth of the gay liberation movement, was also brave and **empowering** for other homosexuals.

Pop Art

During the 1960s, Andy Warhol started to create art from everyday objects – from tins of Campbell's soup to cans of Coca-Cola – and by adapting images

Andy Warhol poses with one of his adaptatons of classic American icons, the Statue of LIberty.

of American icons such as Elvis Presley and Marilyn Monroe. He became a leading figure in what was known as the **Pop Art** movement.

Film-making

Warhol's New York studio, named The Factory, became a gathering point for everyone from artists and filmmakers to celebrities and **drag queens**. Between 1963 and 1968, he made over 60 films, many exploring homosexuality and desire. He was shot in a failed murder attempt in 1968, but lived to inspire further generations of artists from Jean-Michel Basquiat to Damien Hirst.

Name: Andrej Varhola Junior

Born: 6 August 1928 in Pittsburgh, Pennsylvania, USA

Died: 22 February 1987 in New York City, USA

Achievements: Warhol's 1963 silkscreen print 'Eight Elvises' sold for US$100m at auction in 2008, making it one of the most expensive paintings ever sold.

Interesting fact: When Warhol died, a mummified human foot from Ancient Egypt was found among his possessions.

Harvey Milk
The Mayor of Castro Street

Although Harvey Milk knew he was gay from his teens, for many years he chose to remain quiet about his homosexuality. He served as a diving instructor in the US Navy during the Korean War, and after he was **discharged**, lived in New York where he worked first as a teacher, then as a Wall Street investment banker. It was only when Milk became part of a group of **radical** gay friends who lived in the city's Greenwich Village that he started to support the struggle for gay rights.

Name: Harvey Bernard Milk

Born: 22 May 1930 in Woodmere, New York, USA

Died: 27 November 1978 in San Francisco, California, USA

Achievements: Named one of TIME magazine's '100 Heroes and Icons of the 20th Century'. In 2009, Milk was posthumously awarded the Presidential Medal of Freedom by Barack Obama for his contribution to the gay rights movement.

Interesting fact: Sean Penn won an Academy Award for Best Actor in 2009 for his portrayal of Harvey Milk in the film 'Milk'.

In his 11 months in office, Milk was responsible for passing important gay rights legislation.

Living in San Francisco

In 1972, Milk moved to San Francisco and opened a camera shop on Castro Street, in the heart of the gay community. Milk was soon a community spokesperson. In 1973 and 1975 he fought and lost an election for a seat on the San Francisco Board of Supervisors. Although he was unsuccessful, he made an important connection with San Francisco mayor George Moscone, an early supporter of gay rights.

" [Harvey Milk] believed that no sacrifice was too great a price to pay for the cause of human rights. "

President Barack Obama

Harvey Milk has become an icon both for San Francisco's gay community and worldwide.

In office

By 1977, Milk, who was then known as 'the Mayor of Castro Street', won a seat on the San Francisco City-County Board. He took his seat in January 1978, and became the city's first openly gay official, as well as one of the firstly openly gay politicians to be elected in the whole of the United States. Milk helped pass important gay rights legislation for the city, as well as supporting improved childcare and housing programs.

Assassination

Milk's arch-enemy on the board was Dan White, a former policeman who resented the city's growing tolerance for homosexuality. In November 1978, White broke into City Hall, shooting and killing the mayor, Moscone, as well as Milk. White was found guilty of manslaughter rather than murder and was served just five years for his crime. His sentence sparked violent protests among the city's gay community.

MAKING HISTORY

Milk's political career focused on the rights of individuals and the importance of communities to the well-being of cities, and the country as a whole. He died at the height of his popularity, but his legacy lives on.

Frank Kameny
Fighting for fairness

When Frank Kameny was sacked from his job in the US government in 1957 because of his **sexual orientation**, it set in motion a chain of events that would lead to huge advances in gay civil rights.

Fair treatment

Karmeny appealed unsuccessfully against his firing, taking his case as far as the US Supreme Court. In 1961, determined to keep pursuing justice, he co-founded the Mattachine Society of Washington. Kameny and his group formed a **picket line** outside the White House, calling for equal treatment for gay government employees.

Speaking out

In 1963 he started a 10-year campaign to have homosexuality **declassified** as a mental disorder. In 1971 Kameny created the Gay and Lesbian Alliance of Washington DC and became the first openly gay candidate to stand for the US Congress.

Frank Kameny at a 2010 Gay Pride celebration.

Name: Franklin Edward Kameny

Born: 21 May 1925 in New York City, USA

Died: 11 October 2011 in Washington DC, USA

Achievements: Received a formal apology in 2009 from the Office of Personnel Management for his dismissal from the US government, and was given the Theodore Roosevelt Award – the department's highest honour.

Interesting fact: Kameny's original picket signs from his 1965 White House protest are now in the National Museum of American History.

MAKING HISTORY

Inspired by the civil rights movement, Kameny created the slogan 'Gay is Good'. His direct actions brought about fairer treatment for gay people in the workplace and in the military.

Randy Shilts
Groundbreaking journalist

Shilts grew up in small-town America and studied journalism at the University of Oregon, where he was an award-winning editor of the student newspaper. Aged 20 he 'came out' as a gay man – a courageous act at the time, which reflected much of his written work.

In San Francisco

Shilts made no secret of his sexual orientation at job interviews and, despite graduating near the top of his class, found it hard to find full-time work. He was eventually hired by the San Francisco Chronicle to cover national gay politics. His first book, *The Mayor of Castro Street*, covered the assassination of San Francisco politician and personal friend Harvey Milk (see page 13).

Name: Randy Shilts

Born: 8 August 1951 in Davenport, Iowa, USA

Died: 17 February 1994 in Guerneville, California, USA

Achievements: Stonewall Book Award (1987), Outstanding Author Award (1988) from American Society of Journalists and Authors, Lifetime Achievement Award from the National Lesbian and Gay Journalists' Association (1993).

Interesting fact: The film version of 'And The Band Played On' earned 20 award nominations, and won an Emmy for Outstanding Made for Television Movie.

AIDS epidemic

Shilts' second book, *And the Band Played On*, published in 1987, was a **groundbreaking** study of the AIDS **epidemic** that was translated into seven languages and brought him worldwide **recognition**. Before his death from AIDS in 1994, Shilts completed a book on the treatment of gay personnel in the US military, entitled *Conduct Unbecoming*.

The Stonewall Protesters
The spark that ignited gay rights

Name: The Stonewall Inn

Location: Greenwich Village, New York City, USA

Important date: 28 June 1969

Achievements: In 1999 the US Department of the Interior designated the site of the Stonewall Inn as a National Historic Landmark — the first of significance to the **LGBT** community.

Interesting fact: On the 40th anniversary of the Stonewall riots, President Obama declared June 2009 as Lesbian, Gay, Bisexual, and Transgender Pride Month.

The Stonewall Inn today gives little trace of the major part it played in the history of gay rights.

The New York neighbourhoods of Greenwich Village and Harlem have historically had significant homosexual populations, after gay men and women who left their homes to serve in World War I decided to relocate there to live and work in peacetime. However, until the 1950s and 1960s there were very few bars or nightclubs in the city that welcomed openly gay people.

Meeting place

One bar that opened its door to homosexuals was the Mafia-owned Stonewall Inn. The club was basic, with no licence to serve alcohol, no running water behind the bar to wash glasses, and no fire exits, but as the only bar for gay men in New York City where dancing was allowed, it became extremely popular.

Police raid

At 1am on 28 June 1969, uniformed and undercover police officers arrived at the doors of the Stonewall to carry out a raid. By the time the first police vans had arrived to make arrests, thousands of people had gathered outside the bar, and fights broke out between police and bystanders. Bottles were thrown, fires were started, and the police were forced to barricade themselves inside the Stonewall.

A call to action

Riots raged across New York City for several days. More significantly, Greenwich Village residents organized themselves into activist groups to establish more places where gay and lesbian people could be open about their sexuality without fear of arrest. Within six months two gay activist organizations were formed in the city, and three newspapers were launched promoting gay rights. On the one-year anniversary of the raid on the Stonewall Inn, the first Gay Pride marches took place in New York, Chicago and Los Angeles, and within a few years gay rights organizations had spread not only to every major city in American but across the world.

MAKING HISTORY

The police raid on the Stonewall Inn is considered to be the single most important event in the foundation of the gay liberation movement, and the modern fight for gay and lesbian rights.

A Gay Pride celebration passes the Stonewall Inn. A banner on the building says it was 'where Pride began'.

Martina Navratilova

Sporting superstar

Martina Navratilova was often the outsider – US immigrant, **defector** from a **communist** regime, left handed in a right-handed game, and gay in a straight world. She began playing tennis at the age of four, won the Czech national championship at 15, and by 16 had turned professional. Two years later, she defected to the United States.

MAKING HISTORY

As a high-profile openly gay sports personality Navratilova helped put the issue of homosexuality into the public arena, and help build acceptance and understanding of gay and lesbian issues.

Coming out

Navratilova never made a secret of her sexuality, and in 1981 she came out publicly. Her honesty cost her millions of dollars in lost sponsorship deals, but she never once regretted her decision. 'I never thought there was anything strange about being gay,' she wrote in her 1985 autobiography.

Sporting success

Navratilova had won just three major singles titles by the time she was 25, an age at which many players think of retirement. She finished her career with 18, winning 56 Grand Slam championships in total, including doubles and mixed doubles.

Martina Navratilova celebrates one of her many Wimbledon victories, this one against Jana Novotna in 1994.

Name: Martina Subertova (later Navratilova)

Born: 18 October 1956 in Prague, Czechoslovakia

Achievements: Won 18 Grand Slam singles titles, 31 Grand Slam women's doubles titles, and 10 Grand Slam mixed doubles. Named one of the '30 Legends of Women's Tennis' by TIME magazine in 2011.

Interesting fact: Navratilova's grandmother was an international tennis player who once beat a Wimbledon finalist.

Ellen DeGeneres
Queen of comedy

DeGeneres announced her homosexuality on America's number one rated talk show, *The Oprah Winfrey Show*, in 1997 in front of an estimated 9 million viewers. She followed that shortly afterwards with the 'coming out' of her sitcom character in the self-titled *Ellen*, in an episode that proved to be the highest-rated of the series. She even appeared on the cover of *TIME* magazine announcing, 'Yes, I'm gay'.

Hard to accept

Despite not wanting to become, in her words, 'the spokesperson for the gay community', DeGeneres's high-profile announcements led to overwhelming press interest. The obsession with her private life overshadowed her career for a long time, and even led to a period of self-confessed depression.

Finding success

Fortunately, the comedienne bounced back, and by 2003 she had launched a daytime talk show *The Ellen DeGeneres Show*, which recently passed its 1,500th episode and is scheduled to run until at least 2017. When California overturned the same sex marriage ban in 2008, DeGeneres married longtime partner, actress Portia de Rossi. She remains a role model for many people worldwide.

Name: Ellen Lee DeGeneres

Born: 26 January 1958 in Metairie, Louisiana, USA

Achievements: Has won 25 Emmys for her chat show, The Ellen DeGeneres Show. Named by US Secretary of State Hillary Clinton as a Special Envoy for AIDS Awareness (2011).

Interesting fact: Was the first openly gay or lesbian person to host the Oscars (2007).

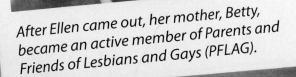
After Ellen came out, her mother, Betty, became an active member of Parents and Friends of Lesbians and Gays (PFLAG).

Sir Elton John

AIDS fundraiser

Elton John's flamboyant stage costumes were a large part of his live performances during the 1970s.

Born Reg Dwight in a suburban council house in north London, Sir Elton John started playing piano at three years old, and by the age of 15 was performing in his local pub for £35 a week. He is now one of the world's most successful recording artists, with 56 Top 40 singles and seven consecutive US number 1 albums. Although he has been married to a woman, he came out as **bisexual** in 1976 and announced he was gay in 1988.

Early years

Sir Elton was an extremely gifted piano player who won a scholarship to the Royal Academy of Music at 11. However, he admits he often missed lessons and spent days riding around London on the underground. In 1967 he met lyricist Bernie Taupin, and the pair began a successful songwriting partnership that has lasted for nearly 50 years and 250 million record sales.

> 66 Imagine walking down the street wondering if this is the day you'll get beaten up, or even killed, simply because of who you are. 99
>
> *Sir Elton John*

Name: Reginald Kenneth Dwight

Born: 25 March 1947 in Pinner, Middlesex, UK

Achievements: Six Grammy Awards, four Brit Awards, and an Oscar for Best Original Song for 'Can You Feel The Love Tonight' in Disney's Lion King. Since 1992 the Elton John AIDS Foundation has raised over US$200m.

Interesting fact: 'Candle in the Wind 1997' has sold over 33m copies worldwide and is the best-selling single in the history of the UK Singles Chart and US Billboard Hot 100.

Crowds watch as Sir Elton John and David Furnish celebrate their civil partnership ceremony in 2005.

Personal life

In 1993, Sir Elton met David Furnish and the pair celebrated their civil partnership in 2005. They have two sons, Zachary and Elijah, from a **surrogate mother**. They also tried to adopt a Ukrainian orphan but were prevented by Ukrainian laws. Sir Elton is also godfather to David Beckham's sons Brooklyn and Romeo.

Fighting AIDS

Since the death of his friend, Queen singer Freddie Mercury, Sir Elton has used his own public profile to help increase awareness of AIDS, and raised millions of pounds to fund research. In 1992 he founded the Elton John AIDS Foundation, which fights to reduce the spread of HIV/AIDS through new healthcare programs, to eliminate discrimination against people fighting the disease, and to provide treatment and support for sufferers. His annual Academy Award Party raises millions of pounds every year to help fund these goals. In 1998, Sir Elton was knighted by Queen Elizabeth II for 'services to music and charitable services'.

Other Gay History Makers

James Baldwin (1924-1987)

A groundbreaking novelist, playwright and poet whose work explored racial and sexual equality. His 1956 novel, *Giovanni's Room*, was criticized for its homosexual content, and appeared many years before equal rights for homosexuals were widely supported in the US.

Elaine Noble (1944-present)

Harvard University graduate Noble was the first openly gay or lesbian candidate elected to public office in the United States. From 1975 to 1979 she served in the Massachusetts House of Representatives. A committed gay rights activist, in 1977 she was invited to discuss LGBT issues with President Carter.

Dan Savage (1964-present)

US journalist who co-founded the It Gets Better internet project in 2010 with his husband, Terry Miller. The site tries to prevent suicides among LGBT teenagers by conveying the message that these teens' lives will improve. Hosting over 50,000 videos, including many from celebrities, which have been viewed over 50 million times, the project was given an Academy of Television Arts Award in 2012 for 'creatively and powerfully utilizing the media to educate and inspire'.

Margarethe Cammermeyer (1942-present)

Cammermeyer was discharged from her job as colonel in the US National Guard for coming out as a lesbian. She fought the case in civil court, where the judge ruled that her dismissal, and the ban on gays and lesbians in the military, was unconstitutional. She returned to work as one of the few openly gay or lesbian personnel in the US military.

Peter Tatchell (1952-present)

An Australian-born political campaigner who moved to London in 1971, Tatchell was a leading member of the Gay Liberation Front (GLF), which protested against police harassment, and the medical classification of homosexuality as an illness. In 1972 he helped to organize Britain's first Gay Pride march, and has been a leading member of OutRage!, a direct action group for LGBT rights.

Matthew Shepard (1976-1998)

Shepard was a University of Wyoming student who was attacked and killed in 1998 because of his sexual orientation. The worldwide attention on his death brought new legislation on hate crime into law. In 2009 President Obama passed the Matthew Shepard Act — a law against hate crimes that was the first to offer legal protections for transgender people.

Timeline

Legacy

1895 Oscar Wilde sent to prison for gross indecency

1924 Henry Gerber forms the Society for Human Rights

1957 Frank Kameny sacked due to his homosexuality

1958 Truman Capote publishes his novel *Breakfast at Tiffany's*

1964 Andy Warhol presents *The American Supermarket Show*

1968 Frank Kameny coins the slogan 'Gay is Good'

1969 The Stonewall Inn is raided by police

1970 The world's first Gay Pride marches

1977 Elaine Noble visits the White House

1978 Harvey Milk murdered

1981 Martina Navratilova comes out as gay

1982 Larry Kramer and friends form the Gay Men's Health Crisis (GMHC)

1987 Larry Kramer co-founds the AIDS Coalition to Unleash Power (ACT UP)

1987 Randy Shilts publishes *And The Band Played On*

1992 Margarethe Cammermeyer discharged from the US National Guard for being a lesbian

1992 Sir Elton John establishes the Elton John AIDS Foundation (EJAF)

2007 Ellen DeGeneres is the first openly gay person to present the Oscars

2009 The Matthew Shepard Act passed, to include hate crimes against homosexuals

2010 It Gets Better Project launched

The legacies of the campaigners in this book live on, not only in their achievements but also through the work of their families and followers:

http://www.stonewall.org.uk
The UK website of the lesbian, gay and bisexual rights charity that is now the largest gay equality organization in Europe.

http://ejaf.com
Established in 1992 to raise money to fund innovative HIV-prevention programs, to try to eliminate the discrimination associated with HIV/AIDS, and to provide support for people living with the disease.

http://www.matthewshepard.org
Founded in December 1998 by Matthew Shepard's parents to support diversity and tolerance in youth organizations, and to ensure equality for all LGBT Americans.

Glossary

Index

bankrupt Unable to pay the debts you owe, having no money.

bisexual A person who is attracted to both men and women.

communist Someone who believes in communism, a way of organizing a country so that all the means of production, such as farms and factories, belong to everyone.

declassified No longer listed or referred to as illegal.

decriminalized Made legal.

defector Someone who leaves a country and becomes a citizen of a new one.

designated Given official recognition or chosen to do a particular job.

discharged Officially released from duty or attendance.

drag queen A man, often a gay man, who dresses as a woman for entertainment.

effeminate When a man behaves or looks similar to a woman.

empowering Making someone feel more confident, more in control of their life.

epidemic The appearance of a disease in a large number of people at the same time.

flamboyant Very confident in behavior, intending to be noticed.

groundbreaking Completely new or different from anything that has gone before.

immunologist A doctor who studies how the body fights disease and infection.

indecency Morally offensive behaviour.

LGBT Stands for 'lesbian, gay, bisexual and transgender'.

picket line A group of people protesting outside a building, and sometimes preventing other workers from going inside.

Pop Art An art movement that began in the US in the 1950s and made use of everyday objects and images from popular culture.

posthumously Happening after a person's death.

radical Describes someone who is an activist with a deeply held belief in a cause such as equal rights for gay people.

recognition The admiration or respect shown for a person's achievements.

sexual orientation An indication of whether someone prefers to have sexual relationships with men, or with women, or with both.

surrogate mother A woman who has a baby for another person who is unable to have their own baby.

thriving Growing, developing successfully.

Malpas Library & Information Centre
2/10/15